The renovation and restoration project was under the architectural direction of Stephen Tilly and Company, specialists in historic preservation. The congregation's building committee devoted tremendous time and effort to seeing the work to completion. They have performed a magnificent and historic service for the congregation of today and for generations to come.

COMMUNAL ENTERPRISES

From 1654 to 1825, Shearith Israel was coextensive with the Jewish community. With the development of new congregations and with the influx of large numbers of Jews to New York in the nineteenth century, Shearith Israel became one institution among many.

The congregation gradually came to terms with the notion that it no longer was the sole authority for Jewish life in New York. While ever protective of its own dignity and traditions, it learned to work with other congregations and agencies in order to advance the well-being of Jews living in the city.

In August 1840, the Jews of New York City held the first mass meeting of American Jews in response to the Damascus Affair. A number of Jews in Damascus, Syria had been falsely accused of murdering a non-Jewish child for ritual purposes, and were to be tried for murder. This heinous charge, known as a blood libel, was an old anti-Jewish canard, used to incite the masses against Jews. When the facts of the case in Damascus came to light, American Jewry responded—perhaps for the first time—as a cohesive national body. The mass meeting in New York was followed by similar gatherings in other American cities.

The New York meeting passed a resolution that was then sent to President Martin Van Buren. The resolution called on the President to "use every possible effort to induce the Pasha of Egypt to manifest more liberal treatment towards his Jewish subjects, not only from the dictates of humanity, but from the obvious policy and justice by which such a course is recommended by the tolerant spirit of the age in which we live." The letter was signed by the leaders of the New York meeting, I. B. Kursheedt and Theodore J. Seixas, both members of prominent Shearith Israel families. The Jewish community received word from the Secretary of State that President Van Buren had indeed already interceded on behalf of the oppressed Jews, and that he was exerting American influence for their release.

During the early 1840s, American Jews became involved in working to alleviate the desperate conditions of Jews in Russia. The president of Shearith Israel attended a community gathering in 1844, signed the resolution on behalf of Russian Jewry, and affixed the seal of the congregation.

Skeptic Lamps

The two-tiered lamps on the north and south walls of the women's gallery are known as "skeptic" lamps. When the synagogue building was constructed in 1897, lighting was provided by gas lamps. Early in the 20th century, with the inception of electric lighting, the Board of Shearith Israel decided to modernize the synagogue by introducing electric lights. Yet, some members resisted this new-fangled suggestion. What if electricity was just a passing fad? What if it proved not to be as reliable as gas lighting?

It was decided, therefore, to have some lamps—the "skeptic" lamps—that would address the doubts of the critics. The top tier of lights would be electrified, and the bottom tier would continue to operate with gas lighting. With the passage of time, it became clear that electricity was a secure

and safe means of lighting the synagogue, and the two-tiered lights were converted entirely to electricity.

Plaque on the exterior of the 70th Street building.

CONGREGATION SHEARITH ISRAEL

This building is a striking example of the monumental neo-American Classic style popular for public and ecclesiastical architecture at the turn of the century. Designed by Brunner & Tryon, it is the fifth synagogue erected by the congregation since 1730. The first building, the earliest synagogue in North America, was located on Mill Street, on the site of what is today 22 South William Street. It provided a permanent house of worship for the Jewish settlers who had been meeting in homes or rented quarters since their arrival in New York in 1654.

Plaque provided by the New York Community Trust 1975

Plaque designating the 70th Street building as a historic monument.

In 1850, Shearith Israel leaders joined with others to protest a treaty between the United States and Switzerland. The Swiss had stipulated that only American Christians could participate in the proposed trade treaty. A committee was formed to circulate a petition to the United States Senate urging that no treaty should be approved that included religious discrimination against American citizens. Four of the thirteen members of this committee were leaders of Shearith Israel.

In 1858, Shearith Israel joined with other Jewish congregations to protest the forcible conversion and kidnapping of a Jewish child in Italy. The child, Edgardo Mortara of Bologna, had been secretly baptized by his Catholic nurse. The Archbishop of Bologna, on orders from the Pope, approved the kidnapping of the child so that he would not revert to Judaism. To the eternal shame of the Catholic church and the Christian nations of the world, Mortara was never returned to his Jewish parents. The protests of world Jewry—and of simple justice and compassion—went unheeded.

These ad hoc efforts at united action by American Jews ultimately led to the establishment of permanent national Jewish organizations. The Board of Delegates of American Israelites was founded in 1859 in order to bring together the diverse organizations of the Jewish community, and to encourage united action. Shearith Israel initially resisted joining. It apparently was concerned that the Board would be overly weighted in favor of the Reform move-

Exterior of the 70th Street building.

ment. Shearith Israel later did join the organization and was represented on it until the Board ceased to function in 1879.

In 1909, the New York Kehillah was established to coordinate work among the Jews of New York. Shearith Israel joined this effort from the beginning. Its early representatives included Dr. David de Sola Pool, L. Napoleon Levy and N. Taylor Phillips—a distinguished group of Shearith Israel's top leadership. The organization, though, did not last too long.

Shearith Israel leaders played roles in the establishment and growth of a variety of Jewish communal organizations including the Union of Orthodox Jewish Congregations of America, the Synagogue Council of America, the New York Board of Rabbis, the Board of Jewish Education, the Federation of Jewish Philanthropies, and others. Members of the congregation participated in national Jewish organizations that developed during the first decades of the twentieth century: the American Jewish Committee, the American Jewish Congress, and the Anti-Defamation League of Bnai Brith.

Dr. Pool noted in his talk in April 1955 that the synagogue was in a world of transition. Its historic experience provided deep roots. The courage and sacrifice of its members over the centuries have created a wellspring of idealism and confidence.

Nearly fifty years later, we can still echo Dr. Pool's words. We have grown and evolved over the years; we need to recognize the new challenges, threats and opportunities that confront us; we need to have an idealistic and purposive vision for the future. The American Jewish community has weathered three hundred and fifty years. It has enjoyed wonderful times, and has endured some very difficult times. We are still here to tell our story. We are a vital, dynamic and idealistic community. We owe much to the earlier generations of Jews in America; we owe much to current generations of devoted Jews. We owe much to the American system of government and to our non-Jewish fellow citizens.

On this historic occasion of our three hundred and fiftieth anniversary in America, we bow our heads in gratitude to the Almighty. We thank Him for having sustained us and maintained us and granted us the privilege of reaching this special time.

In closing his remarks at the consecration of the Second Mill Street Synagogue on April 17, 1818, Mordecai M. Noah offered a prayer, with which we close this book. "May we prove ever worthy of His blessing; may He look down from His heavenly abode, and send us peace and comfort; may He instill in our minds a love of country, of friends, and of all mankind. Be just, therefore, and fear not. That God who brought us out of the land of Egypt, who walked before us like 'a cloud by day and a pillar of fire by night,' will never desert His people Israel."

APPENDICES

OPPOSITE:
*One of the rimonim
presented to Shearith Israel
in 1897 by Hazzan
Abraham Haim Nieto.*

167

APPENDIX A

APPENDIX B

SEVENTEENTH-CENTURY
MEMBERS OF SHEARITH ISRAEL

The following material is reprinted from *An Old Faith in the New World*, by David and Tamar de Sola Pool, pp. 468–9.

WHEN AFTER 1664 Nieuw Amsterdam became New York, we see Asser Levy and Jacob Israel signing an oath of allegiance to the new government in 1668. Two years later, David Machoro appears on the scene. All records that may have been kept by the Jewish congregation in New York in the seventeenth century have disappeared. In order to learn what Jews were in the congregation in those days, we have to search through public records, such as the names of those given letters of denization and those admitted as free-men, tax lists, and records of court procedures in such matters as the adjudication of business claims. That tireless student of American Jewish history, Samuel Oppenheim, delighted to search laboriously through all such documents, and we owe most of the names which follow to his papers which are now in the archives of the American Jewish Historical Society. Among the Jews who made up the Jewish community in New York in the last four decades of the seventeenth century were David (1681) and Raphael (1694) Abendana, and Mordecai Abendanon, who died of smallpox in 1690; Moses Aboab, a merchant who in 1684 received a license to trade; Isaac Asher; Simon Bonam (1687); David Pardo (1684) and Joseph Pardo (d. 1690), and Shearith Israel's rabbi and merchant Saul Brown-Pardo (1685), and his wife Esther (d. 1708); Daniel Campanal (1697); Isaac Cotinho (1676); an Italian Jew, Rabba Couty (1666–1674; Isaac da Costa (1686); Benjamin and Esther de Casseres (1689); Isaac Cohen de Lara (1699); Shearith Israel's rabbi and merchant Abraham de Lucena (1699); Benjamin Bueno de Mesquita (d. 1683), who is the first known to us to be buried in the Chatham Square Cemetery purchased in 1682, and Joseph Bueno de Mesquita (1682) and his wife, Rachel Doval(e); Jacob de Robles and David and Bienvenida de Robles, who had been forced to leave France on account of persecution, and who on their arrival in 1687 petitioned for letters of denization and permission to bring ashore goods which they had on board ship; Isaac Fernandes Dias, who in 1700 is on record as voting for a city alderman, and his assistant; Jacob do Porto (1697); Isaac Gabay Faro (1686) and Esther Bueno de Mesquita, his wife, and their daughter Bilhah (d. 1694) ; Benjamin Franks, a jeweler, formerly resident of Barbados and Jamaica, who sailed away from the city in September, 1696, on Captain Kidd's vessel and survived the captain's piratical adventures; Bianca Henriques Granada, who died in the smallpox epidemic of 1690, and Isaac and Sarah Henriques Granada; the butcher Isaac Henriques, who became a free man in 1688; Elijah Ilhoa, who died in 1699, and whose grave had to be moved a century and a half later from the Chatham Square graveyard to that on 21st Street; Abraham Isaacs (1699), Jacob Isaacs, the butcher Joseph Isaacs, who became a freeman in 1698, and who died in 1737, and his wife; the widow Rifka Isaacs; the soapmaker Benjamin Israel (1699), who is also recorded as a city voter, and Jacob Israel (1675); Moses Levi (1691), who in 1695 was granted denization rights and admitted as a freeman; an unsuccessful butcher, Ansell Samuel Levy (1685), and his wife, Margaret, who when he married her was the widow of the community leader Asser Levy; Moses Levy (d. 1728), the parnas of the community when the decision was made to build the Mill Street Synagogue, his wife Grace Mears Levy, and his brother Samuel Levy characterized by James Alexander as a most honest man and a man of *most* easy temper, and his wife Rachel (d. 1732), daughter of Asher Michalls de Paul; Isaac Rodrigues Marques (1695) and Rebecca Rodrigues Marques (d. 1697); Abraham de Sosa Mendes (1683); Asher and Rebecca Michalls (de Paul); Isaac and Sarah Naphtali; the learned young merchant Joseph Tores Nunes, who died in 1704 when only thirty years of age; David D. Robles (1696); and David Valentine van der Wilder.

APPENDIX C

MEMBERS OF SHEARITH ISRAEL AS RECORDED IN A 1720–21 RECORD BOOK OF NATHAN SIMSON

This information is drawn from the article by Jacob R. Marcus, "The Oldest Known Synagogue Record Book of Continental North America, 1720–1721," page 232.

SEPHARDIM	ASHKENAZIM
Abraham (Haim) de Lucena	Abraham bar Isaac (Abraham Isaacs)
Abraham Pinto	Asher Myer(s)
Abraham Burgos	Baruch Judah
Jacob Louzada	Benjamin Wolf
Abraham Gomez Caseres	Nathan Simson
Benjamin Pacheco	Eliezer bar Judah
Daniel Nunes (da Costa)	Jacob bar Higuell
David Angell	Isaac Cohen
Isaac de Medina	Jacob Franks
Lewis Moses Gomez	Isaac Jacobs
Mordecai Gomez	Joseph Simson
Moses Lopez da Fonseca	Moses Levy
Abraham Gutieres	Moses Michell
Moses Cohen Peixotto	Moses Sevy (Hart)
Samuel Coronell	Nehemiah Marks
	Solomon Michaell
	Simon Moses
	Solomon Myers
	Baruch Levy
	Michael Asher
	Isaac Polack
	Joseph Isaacs

APPENDIX D

Soldiers and patriots of the American Revolution
whose graves are decorated on Memorial Day

INTERRED IN THE ST. JAMES PLACE (CHATHAM SQUARE) CEMETERY OF CONGREGATION SHEARITH ISRAEL.

(As listed in *An Old Faith in the New World*, by David and Tamar de Sola Pool, pp. 504–5.)

SOLOMON MYERS COHEN, 1745–1796

Merchant. Son of Abraham Cohen. Private in Captain Isaac Austin's 5th Battalion, Upper Delaware Ward, Pa. Militia; also Private in Captain Thomas Bradford's Company, 1st Battalion, Philadelphia, Pa. Militia, and later in Captain Andrew Geyer's Company, in Colonel William Will's 3rd Battalion, Pa. Militia. Died February 15, 1796.

JACOB HART, 1746–1822

Merchant. Born in Germany, son of Jacob Hart. Associator. Advanced money to General Lafayette to clothe and feed his troops; thanked by Congress May 24, 1781. Died May 9, 1822.

DAVID HAYS, 1732–1812

Merchant. Born in New Rochelle, N.Y., in March 1732, son of Jacob Hays. Associator. His house and store were destroyed by Tories in July 1779, while he was away in Long Island with colonial troops. He also served in the New York Militia at Braddock's Field in the French and Indian War. Died at Mt. Pleasant, N.Y., Oct. 18, 1812.

JOSHUA ISAACS, 1744–1810

Merchant. Born in New York City, N.Y., posthumous son of Joshua Isaacs. President of the New York Jewish community 1799. Private in Captain Joseph Hubley's 3rd Company, Colonel James Ross' 8th Battalion, Lancaster Co., Pa. Militia, and later in Captain Hubley's 1st Company of that Battalion. Died in New York City, February 17, 1810.

BENJAMIN JACOBS, 1737–1811

Merchant. Born in Curacao, West Indies. Son of Jacob Jacobs. Private in Captain George Brown's 1st Company, Lieutenant Colonel Will Nichols' 1st Battalion, 5th Regiment, Philadelphia, Pa. Militia, and in Captain Fred Shull's 3rd Company, 1st Battalion, 5th Regiment of Philadelphia, Pa., Militia. Signer of Bills of Credit for Continental Congress. Died in New York City, December 15, 1811.

MOSES JUDAH, 1735–1822

Merchant. Born in New York City, son of Baruch Judah. Private in Captain Thomas Bradford's Company, 1st Battalion of the Philadelphia Militia. Died in New York City, September 25, 1822.

ELEAZAR LEVY, ?–1811

Merchant. Son of Hayman Levy. Private, Captain Samuel McLean's Company, 1st Battalion, Pa., Militia. Died in New York City, February 12,1811.

HAYMAN LEVY, 1721–1789

Merchant. Born in Hanover, Germany, January 25, 1721, son of Moses Isaac Levy. Private in Captain Adam Foulk's Company 4th Battalion, Pa. Militia. Signer of Non-Importation Resolutions of 1770. Died in New York City, August 20, 1789.

ISAAC MOSES, 1742–1818

Merchant, ship owner. Born in Germany, son of Moses David. Private in Captain Andrew Burkhard's Company, in Colonel William Will's 3rd Battalion, Philadelphia, Pa. Militia. Signer of Bills of Credit for Continental Congress. Died at Mount Listen, New York City, April 16, 1818.

MYER MYERS, 1723–1795

Son of Solomon Myers. Silversmith. President of the New York Jewish community 1759 and 1770. Associator.

SIMON NATHAN, 1746–1822

Merchant. Born in Frome, England, son of Judah Nathan. Private in Captain Andrew Geyer's 3rd Company, Colonel William Will's 4th Battalion, Philadelphia, Pa. Militia; also provided large sums of money for the Revolutionary cause. Died in New York City, September 8, 1822.

JOSEPH NATHANS, 1738–1798

Merchant. Born in Germany, 1738, son of Nathan Jacob. Private in Captain Jacob Buss' Company, in Lieutenant Colonel Christian Shouse's Battalion, Northampton County, Pa. Militia; Private in Captain Henry Alshouse's 5th Company, Colonel Roup's rod Battalion, Northampton County, Pa. Militia. Private in Captain Abraham Horn's Company, Easton, Northampton County, Pa. Militia. Died in New York City, October 1, 1798.

MANUEL NOAH, 1755–1821

Merchant. Born in Mannheim, Germany, son of Noah. Private in Captain Thomas Willis' 7th Company, Lieutenant Colonel John Shee's 1st Battalion, Philadelphia, Pa. Militia. Died in New York City, January 11, 1821.

JONAS PHILLIPS, 1736–1803

Merchant. Born in Busick, in Rhenish Prussia, Germany, son of Aaron Uri Phillips. Private in Captain John Linton's Company, Colonel William Bradford's Battalion, Philadelphia, Pa. Militia. Signer of Non-Importation Resolutions of 1770. Died in Philadelphia, Pa., January 19, 1803.

ABRAHAM RODRIGUES RIVERA, 1761–1813

Merchant. Born in Newport, R.I. in December 1762, son of Jacob Rodrigues Rivera. Private in Newport Artillery Company, Rhode Island Militia. Died in New York City, January 10, 1823.

BENJAMIN MENDES SEIXAS, 1748–1817

Merchant. Born in New York City, on January 28, 1748, son of Isaac Mendes Seixas, Third Lieutenant in Fusiliers' Company, 1st Battalion, New York Militia. Died in New York City, August 16, 1817.

GERSHOM MENDES SEIXAS, 1745–1816

Minister of the Spanish and Portuguese Synagogue. Born in New York City on January 14, 1745, son of Isaac Mendes Seixas, Associator. Preached the American cause in the Revolution, closed the synagogue and removed the holy scrolls to Stratford, Connecticut, when the British occupied New York City. Died in New York City, July 2, 1816.

SOLOMON SIMSON, 1738–1801

Merchant. Born in New York City, son of Joseph Simson. Supplied cannon to New York Militia; contributed lead for making bullets; member of House of Delegates of New York. Died in Yonkers, N.Y., January 17, 1801.

INTERRED IN THE ELEVENTH STREET CEMETERY
OF CONGREGATION SHEARITH ISRAEL

EPHRAIM HART, 1747–1825

Broker. Born in Fuerth, Germany, son of Samuel Hart. Private in Pennsylvania Militia, 1781–1786. Father of Dr. Joel Hart President of the New York community in 1794. A founder of the New York stock exchange. Died in New York City, July 16, 1825.

INTERRED IN THE TWENTY-FIRST STREET CEMETERY
OF CONGREGATION SHEARITH ISRAEL

ISAAC NUNES CARDOZO, 1737–1823

Born in London, England, son of Aaron Nunes Cardozo. Private in Charleston, S. Carolina Militia. Died in New York City, July 22, 1832.

DANIEL GOMEZ, 1759–1784

Son of Moses D. Gomez. Private in Captain John Corrush's Company in the Fourth Battalion of the Philadelphia Militia. Died August 27, 1784, and interred in the Chatham Square Cemetery. His grave transferred in 1856.

ABRAHAM JUDAH, 1714–1784

Son of Uriah Judah. Private, Dock Ward Company, Philadelphia, PA Militia, 1776. Died in New York City, September 2, 1784, and interred in the Chatham Square Cemetery. His grave, transferred in 1856.

APPENDIX E

CHRONOLOGY

1654 Twenty-three Jews arrive in New Amsterdam in September, the beginning of Jewish settlement in North America.

1664 The British take control of New Amsterdam, and rename it New York.

1683 Date of oldest tombstone, that of Benjamin Bueno de Mesquita, in Shearith Israel's Chatham Square Cemetery.

1695 Map of New York City by John Miller indicates location of a synagogue on Mill Street. At that time, a rented house served as the synagogue.

1702 Saul Pardo, first known hazzan of Shearith Israel, begins service.

1706 c. Adoption of "certain wholesome rules and restrictions," for the governance of the Congregation.

1728 Adoption of new Shearith Israel constitution, composed in Portuguese and English.

1730 Consecration of Shearith Israel's first Mill Street Synagogue, the first synagogue building constructed in North America.

1733 Jewish community forms in Savannah, Georgia.

1740 Jewish community forms in Philadelphia, Pennsylvania.

1749 c. Jewish community forms in Charleston, South Carolina.

1763 Consecration of the synagogue building in Newport, Rhode Island, later to become known as the Touro Synagogue.

1768 Reverend Gershom Mendes Seixas begins tenure as hazzan of Shearith Israel.

Establishment of Congregation Shearith Israel of Montreal, Canada.   179

1776	The Declaration of Independence of the United States on July 4.
	Reverend Gershom Mendes Seixas and other patriots flee New York City in September, rather than live under British control.
1783	Removal of British troops from New York in November.
1784	Shearith Israel is incorporated according to New York State's new law for the incorporation of religious societies.
1789	A parade is held in Philadelphia in honor of the new United States Constitution. Tables with kasher food are prepared for the Jewish participants.
1791	Jewish community forms in Richmond, Virginia.
1797	Shearith Israel adopts an official seal.
1798	Death of Walter Judah, a twenty year old medical student who died while aiding those stricken with yellow fever.
1800	Sampson Simson delivers graduation address in Hebrew, upon graduation from Columbia University.
1801	Myer Polonies leaves a bequest to Shearith Israel, leading to the establishment of a Talmud Torah for the religious education of the community's children.
1802	Founding of the Hebra Hased va Amet.
1804	Purchase of land for cemetery on 11th Street.
1805	Shearith Israel adopts new constitution and by-laws, which still govern the congregation today.
1806	Moses Judah is elected to the Standing Committee of the New York Manumission Society, whose goal was to arrange for the freedom of slaves.
1812	Uriah P. Levy, at age 20, begins his naval career in the War of 1812; later goes on to become a Commodore.
1813	Mordecai Manuel Noah is appointed U.S. Consul to Tunis by President James Madison.
1816	Moses Levi Maduro Peixotto is appointed hazzan of Shearith Israel.
1818	Consecration of Shearith Israel's second Mill Street Synagogue.

1825   Establishment of a second Jewish congregation in New York, Bnai Jeshurun, which followed the Ashkenazic rite.

Mordecai Manuel Noah launches project to establish a Jewish colony in Ararat, NY.

1828   Isaac Benjamin Seixas is appointed as hazzan of Shearith Israel.

The founding of the Hebrew Relief Society.

1829   Establishment of new cemetery on 21st Street.

1834   Consecration of Shearith Israel's Crosby Street Synagogue.

1836   Uriah P. Levy purchases Monticello from the heirs of Thomas Jefferson. Monticello remained in the possession of the Levy family until 1923.

1839   Reverend Jacques Judah Lyons is appointed as hazzan of Shearith Israel.

1840   Mass meeting of Jews in New York City to demand the intervention of the American government on behalf of oppressed Jews in Damascus, Syria. Similar meetings followed in Philadelphia, Charleston, Cincinnati, Savannah and Richmond.

1847   Meeting at Shearith Israel to raise funds for Irish famine relief.

1852   Founding of Jews' Hospital, later to be called Mt. Sinai Hospital.

1860   Consecration of Shearith Israel's 19th Street Synagogue.

1865   Memorial services at Shearith Israel for Abraham Lincoln.

1877   Dr. Henry Pereira Mendes begins tenure as Minister of Shearith Israel.

1885   Chapel built at Shearith Israel's Cypress Hills cemetery by Vaux and Radford.

1896   The establishment of the Sisterhood of the Spanish and Portuguese Synagogue.

1897   Maud Nathan becomes President of the Consumers' League, an office she held for twenty years.

Consecration of Shearith Israel's 70th Street Synagogue, the current home of the Congregation.

1898	The Union of Orthodox Jewish Congregations of America is founded largely through the efforts of Rev. Dr. Henry Pereira Mendes.
1899	Barnard College opens as a result of the efforts of Annie Nathan Meyer, who served as a lifelong trustee of the college.
1903	A plaque with Emma Lazarus' poem "The New Colossus" is affixed to the Statue of Liberty.
1907	Dr. David de Sola Pool is appointed Assistant Minister to Dr. Mendes. He went on to become Minister and then Minister Emeritus, and was associated with Shearith Israel until his death in 1970.
1910	Moise Gadol publishes the first issue of La America, a weekly Ladino newspaper in New York that ran from 1910 to 1925.
1913	The Sisterhood opens a Settlement House on Orchard Street on the Lower East Side of New York City to assist Sephardic immigrants.
1918	The Sisterhood opens a larger Settlement House on Eldridge Street.
1919	Founding of the Shearith Israel League.
1921	Dedication of four bronze lamps in the Main Sanctuary, in memory of four congregants who were killed in action during World War I.
1929	Dr. David de Sola Pool leads in the establishment of the Union of Sephardic Congregations.
1930s–1940s	Relief efforts for victims of Nazism and Fascism in Europe, and assistance to refugees arriving in the United States.
1932	Justice Benjamin Nathan Cardozo is appointed to the United States Supreme Court.
1941	Monument known as the Triumvirate of Patriots, featuring Revolutionary War heroes George Washington, Robert Morris and Haym Salomon, is dedicated in Chicago.
1942	Dr. Louis C. Gerstein is appointed as Assistant Minister to Dr. Pool.
1946	Reverend Abraham Lopes Cardozo begins his tenure as hazzan.
	Touro Synagogue in Newport is proclaimed a National Historic site.
1954	Observance of Shearith Israel's (and American Jewry's) tercentenary year.

1961   Set of rimonim fashioned in the model of the Liberty Bell is presented to Shearith Israel in honor of the 70th birthday of Judge Edgar J. Nathan, Jr. These rimonim symbolize the harmonious blending of Jewish and American traditions.

1963   Haham Dr. Solomon Gaon is appointed chairman of the Sephardic studies program at Yeshiva University.

1969   Rabbi Marc D. Angel is appointed as Student Minister, becoming Assistant Minister the following year. He is appointed Minister in 1977, while Dr. Gerstein becomes Senior Minister.

1972   The American Sephardi Federation is reconstituted at a convention held at Shearith Israel.

1978   Rabbi Marc D. Angel leads in the establishment of Sephardic House, a national organization dedicated to fostering Sephardic history and culture.

1995   Rabbi Hayyim Angel is appointed Education Director. In 1997 he becomes Assistant Minister, and in 2001 is appointed Associate Minister.

2002   Reconsecration of the Main Sanctuary after a major project of restoration and renovation.

2004   The Congregation celebrates its 350th Anniversary—the 350th Anniversary of the founding of the American Jewish community.

BIBLIOGRAPHY

——◆——

THE PRIMARY SOURCE MATERIAL for this book was drawn from the archives of Congregation Shearith Israel: the 1728 Portuguese-English Record Book; the volumes of the Minutes of the Trustees; the Minutes of the Oriental Committee of the Sisterhood; and other documents in the Shearith Israel collection.

Records from the Shearith Israel archives have been published in the *Publications of the American Jewish Historical Society,* vol. 21 (1913), and vol. 27 (1920).

The authoritative history of Shearith Israel is *An Old Faith in The New World: Portrait of Shearith Israel 1654–1954*, by David and Tamar de Sola Pool, Columbia University Press, New York, 1955. Biographies of those buried in the early cemeteries of Shearith Israel are found in *Portraits Etched in Stone*, by David de Sola Pool, Columbia University Press, New York, 1952.

Basic studies relating to the first two centuries of Shearith Israel's history are *The Rise of the Jewish Community of New York* by Hyman Grinstein, Jewish Publication Society of America, Philadelphia, 1947; and *A Time for Planting: The First Migration 1654–1820,* by Eli Faber, The Johns Hopkins University Press, Baltimore and London, 1992.

The following is a selection of books and articles that have been helpful in the preparation of this book:

OPPOSITE:
Portico at the front entrance to the synagogue on Central Park West.

Adelman, David C., "They Broke In—To Pray," *Rhode Island Jewish Historical Notes,* vol. 2, no. 1, April 1958, pp. 226–237.

Angel, Hayyim, ed., *Seeking Good, Speaking Peace: Collected Essays Of Rabbi Marc D. Angel,* Ktav Publishing House, Hoboken, 1994.

Angel, Marc D., *La America: The Sephardic Experience in the United States,* Jewish Publication Society, Philadelphia, 1982.

_____, "New York's Early Jews: Some Myths and Misconceptions," in a pamphlet published by Jewish Historical Society of New York, 1976, pp. 18–27.

_____, ed., *Rabbi David de Sola Pool: Selections from Six Decades of Sermons, Addresses and Writings,* Union of Sephardic Congregations, 1980.

_____, "The New Amsterdam Contract and Jewish Traditional Values in the Practices of Self-Help", paper delivered to the National Conference of Jewish Communal Service, June 6, 1975.

_____, "The Religious Vision of Rev. Dr. Henry Pereira Mendes," in *From Strength to Strength*, ed. M. D. Angel, Sepher Hermon Press, New York, 1998, pp. 21–28.

_____, "The Sephardim of the United States: An Exploratory Study," *American Jewish Yearbook 1973*, Jewish Publication Society Of America, Philadelphia, pp. 77–138.

_____, "Thoughts About Early American Jewry," *Tradition*, vol. 16 (Fall 1976), pp. 16–23.

_____, *Voices in Exile*, Ktav Publishing House, Hoboken, 1991.

Angel, Ronda, "Architecture and Visual Arts of the Spanish and Portuguese Synagogue of New York City," in *Haham Gaon Memorial Volume*, ed. M. D. Angel, Sephardic House, New York, 1997, pp. 223–233.

Arbell, Mordechai, *The Jewish Nation of the Caribbean: The Spanish-Portuguese Jewish Settlements in the Caribbean and the Guianas*, Gefen Publishing House, Jerusalem, 2002.

Berger, Maurice, "A. Brunner's Spanish and Portuguese Synagogue: Issues of Reform and Reaffirmation in Late Nineteenth-Century America," *Arts Magazine*, vol. 54, pp. 164–167.

Blau, Joseph and Baron, Salo, *The Jews of the United States, 1790–1840: A Documentary History,* 3 vols., Columbia University Press, New York, 1963.

Dexter, F. B., ed., *The Literary Diary of Ezra Stiles*, New York, 1901.

Ezratty, Harry A., *500 Years in the Jewish Caribbean: the Spanish and Portuguese Jews in the West Indies,* Omni Arts Publishers, Baltimore, 2002.

Gutstein, Morris, *The Story of the Jews of Newport*, Bloch, New York, 1936.

Hershkowitz, Leo and Meyer, Isidore, eds., *Letters of the Franks Family (1733–1748),* American Jewish Historical Society, Waltham, 1968.

Hertz, Emanuel, ed., *Abraham Lincoln: The Tribute of the Synagogue,* Bloch Publishing Company, New York, 1927.

Johnson, Paul, *A History of the American People,* Harper Collins, New York, 1997.

_____ , *A History of the Jews*, Harper Perennial, New York, 1988.

Lazarus, Emma, *An Epistle to the Hebrews,* ed. Morris U. Schappes, Jewish Historical Society of New York, New York, 1987.

_____ , *Emma Lazarus: Selections from her Poetry and Prose,* ed. Morris U. Schappes, Emma Lazarus Federation of Jewish Women's Clubs, New York, 1982.

Leepson, Marc, *Saving Monticello,* Free Press, New York, 2001.

Libo, Kenneth and Hoffman, Abigail Kursheedt, *The Seixas-Kursheedts and the Rise of Early American Jewry,* Bloch Publishing Company, New York, 2001.

Marcus, Jacob R., *American Jewry—Documents—Eighteenth Century*, Hebrew Union College Press, Cincinnati, 1959.

_____ , *Early American Jewry*, 2 vols., Jewish Publication Society, Philadelphia, 1951–53.

_____ , "Handsome Young Priest in the Black Gown: The Personal World of Gershom Seixas," *Hebrew Union College Annual,* vol. 40–41 (1969–70), pp. 409–67.

_____ , "The Jew and the American Revolution: A Bicentennial Documentary," *American Jewish Archives*, vol. 27, (1975), pp. 103–257.

_____ , "The Oldest Known Synagogue Record Book of Continental North America", in *In The Time of Harvest*, ed. D. J. Silver, Macmillan, New York, 1963, pp.227–235.

_____ , *United States Jewry 1776–1985*, Wayne State University Press, Detroit, 1989.

Markens, Isaac, "Lincoln and the Jews," *Publications of the American Jewish Historical Society,* vol. 17, pp. 142–43.

Menken, Alice Davis, *On the Side of Mercy*, Covici, Friede, Publishers, New York, 1933.

Meyer, Isidore, "The Hebrew Oration of Sampson Simson, 1800," *Publications of the American Jewish Historical Society*, vol. 46 (1956), pp. 51–58.

Nathan, Maud, *Once Upon a Time and Today*, Arno Press, New York, 1974.

_____, *The Story of an Epoch-Making Movement,* Doubleday, Page and Company, New York, 1926.

Noah, Mordecai, *Discourse, Delivered at the Consecration of the Synagogue of K.K. Shearith Israel,* New York, 1818.

_____, *Discourse on the Restoration of the Jews*, 1845, Reprinted in *Call to America to Build Zion,* Arno Press, New York, 1977.

Phillips, N. Taylor, "Items Relating to the History of the Jews of New York," *Publications of the American Jewish Historical Society,* vol. 9 (1903), pp. 149–161.

_____, "The Congregation Shearith Israel," *Publications of the Jewish Historical Society of America*, vol. 6 (1897), pp. 123–140.

_____, "Unwritten History," *American Jewish Archives*, vol. 6 (1954), pp. pp. 77–104.

Pool, David de Sola, "Early Relations Between Palestine and American Jewry," *Brandeis Avukah Annual*, 1932, pp. 536–548.

_____, *H. Pereira Mendes, A Biography*, New York, 1938.

_____, "Religious and Cultural Phases of American Jewish History," *Publications of the American Jewish Historical Society*, vol. 39 (1950), pp. 291–301.

Reznikoff, Charles and Engelman, Uriah, *The Jews of Charleston,* Jewish Publication Society, Philadelphia, 1950.

Rosenbaum, Jeanette, *Myer Myers, Goldsmith 1723–1795*, Jewish Publication Society, Philadelphia, 1954.

Rubin, Saul, *Third to None: The Saga of Savannah Jewry, 1733–1983*, S. J. Rubin, Savannah, 1983.

Salomon, Herman P., "K.K. Shearith Israel's First Language: Portuguese," *Tradition*, vol. 30 (Fall 1995), pp. 74–84.

Sarna, Jonathan D., *Jacksonian Jew: The Two Worlds of Mordecai Noah,* Holmes and Meier Publishers, New York and London, 1981.

Schappes, Morris U., *A Documentary History of the Jews of the United States 1654–1875,* Schocken, New York, 1971.

Serageldin, I, Shluger, E., and Martin-Brown, J., eds. *Historic Cities And Sacred Sites: Cultural Roots for Urban Futures,* The World Bank, Washington D. C., 2001.

Swetschinski, Daniel, *Reluctant Cosmopolitans: the Portuguese Jews Of Seventeenth-Century Amsterdam,* Littman Library of Jewish Civilization, London, 2000.

Swierenga, Robert, *The Forerunners: Dutch Jewry in the North American Diaspora,* Wayne State University Press, Detroit, 1994.

Urofsky, Melvin I., *The Levy Family and Monticello, 1834–1923,* The Thomas Jefferson Foundation, Monticello Monograph Series, 2001.

Whiteman, Maxwell, *Copper for America: The Hendricks Family And a National Industry, 1755–1939,* Rutgers University Press, New Brunswick, 1971.

Wischnitzer, Rachel, *Synagogue Architecture in the United States: History and Interpretation*, Jewish Publication Society, Philadelphia, 1955.

Wolf, Edwin and Whiteman, Maxwell, *The History of the Jews of Philadelphia from Colonial Times to the Age of Jackson,* Jewish Publication Society, Philadelphia, 1957.

Wolff, Frances Nathan, *Four Generations: My Life and Memories of New York for Over Eighty Years,* New York, 1939 (reprinted 1987).

Young, Bette Roth, *Emma Lazarus in Her World,* Jewish Publication Society, Philadelphia, 1995.